A DAILY

FROM

GROUCHY

Great

Finding Joy in
the Journey of Motherhood

Ruth Schwenk

WITH THEBETTERMOM.COM CONTRIBUTOR TEAM

Table of Contents

Hi, Friends!

This has been an incredible journey of The Better Mom website and ministry. We are so humbled and amazed by God's work through *The Better Mom* blog *(www.thebettermom.com), The Better Mom* podcast and *The Better Mom* book.

I am excited to share with you a great resource for personal use, or group study. A few years ago, we did a series on The Better Mom called, *Grouchy to Great*. We have taken those posts, added devotional/discussion questions, and assembled it all into an easy to use devotional. Grab a journal and study through it by yourself, or gather some girlfriends and study together!

All of us as moms struggle to keep it all together sometimes. The battle for Jesus to reign in our hearts and through our emotions is a fight we all face every day. The good news is that we don't have to battle alone. This is a resource filled with real life stories to strengthen and encourage you that the battle can be won by God's grace and wisdom. We trust it will be a blessing to you as you seek to walk in greater joy and peace.

I want to personally thank you friend, for joining our community and sharing life with us. I pray that this book will be a tool that God uses in your life, for many years to come.

I also invite you to subscribe to *The Better Mom* online community at *thebettermom.com* and receive free downloadable gifts plus a list of our most popular resources to further support your Grouchy to Great journey.

If you are already a subscriber of The Better Mom, you can see these resources linked in the bottom of our emails.

Blessings,

Ruth Schwenk

The Lord is my strength and my shield;
my heart trusts in him, and he
helps me.
My heart leaps for joy,
and with my song I praise him.
Psalm 28:7

Day 1

Mom is Crabby...Again?
by Ruth Schwenk

Dreadful Sunday morning mistake #1: I chose getting ready BEFORE having my cup of coffee.

You see, we were running just a wee bit late for church. (As usual.) Honestly, it never fails: no matter what time we wake up, we end up scurrying around the house. (Can anyone relate?)
And because my husband is already at the church, getting four kids dressed, fed, brushed, combed, presentable and happy falls to me. Not that I mind...

But doing all this BEFORE a cup of coffee? Let's just say that isn't a wise choice. Ever. Which leads me to...

Dreadful Sunday morning mistake #2: While backing out of the garage, I announced to my four children, "I just want everyone to know that I did NOT have my coffee this morning."

Yes, on this particular Sunday morning, after we had all finally made it into the car (a BIG accomplishment, and I know you understand this 100%), I declared my disgruntlement and displeasure.

My 10, 8, 6 and 4-year-old did not have to guess: Mom was crabby. Again.

Really, we should have been singing a song of victory that we were actually IN the car, backing out of the garage and on our way. But no, I had to announce my annoyance to the world.

Thankfully, I hadn't acted too ridiculously that morning, and my proclamation (and to be fair, my subsequent apology) was greeted with grins and chuckles as ifto say, "Oh Mom, that's okay." They loved me in my weakness, and I am grateful.

But what is the deal with the crabby attitude?

Obviously, I am NOT talking about my children's attitude; I am talking about my own!

I know you understand. So I wonder...

What is it that is making us so downcast? Why do we sometimes slip into anger too easily? Why do we unleash our attitudes on our children? And—most importantly—how can we change?

The reason I asked the questions above is because every time we talk about anger or grouchiness at The Better Mom *(www. thebettermom.com)*, you respond. Many times you are asking for prayer and help to overcome the anger that so easily wells up and spills out in your home. The comments flood in with all of the reasons you feel grouchy, discouraged, and angry.

Here are just a few of your responses:

> *"I feel like this every morning. I find myself screaming at my boys, I hardly ever get to say goodbye to my husband properly and then when I get 5 minutes to myself I can't understand why or what makes me get to that point. I feel like the only way they listen to me is when I shout but it makes me so sad to see their faces when I shout."*

> *"I so struggle with the crabbiness, exhaustion, etc. I know that I struggle to find time (more than a few minutes here or there) to breathe—relax—do something fun. Everything feels like work. I love my kids—but I hate feeling crabby, angry—having the little things make me crazy. I spend*

time in God's word daily—but it's not enough. I don't know what the answer is…but wish I knew how to rid this crabby, poor attitude."

"I definitely struggle with this. I have a 3 year old and a baby, which is challenging enough some days, but I have also had marriage problems for the entirety of our nearly 4 years of marriage. I think feeling alone because of that makes everything that much harder. It's difficult to not have a partner I can trust, so I feel like I'm responsible for everything in our house, and that is so tiring. Throw in a cranky 3 year old and a baby that's up all night, and it's a recipe for disaster. I'm honestly not sure how to fix it."

"Oh boy! This one hit home. I can be guilty of this so many times, especially as you shared—when in a hurry. For me personally, it really comes down to my expectations not being met."

"For me, it is being overwhelmed and feeling burnt out. I am a homeschooling stay at home Mom. So there are days I literally do not get a break."

"I know it is ME and not them! God has blessed me with awesome little boys that I fail daily. It is my poor attitude that no matter the reading and prayer I cant seem to shake and get past. I feel that I have no life, no place, no purpose and the day in day out same old same old has really taken its toll. I feel stuck and it is reflected in my behavior towards my family, friends, and now complete strangers."

Response

1. How do you relate to Ruth's story or some of the comments from readers?

2. As we begin this study, list the emotions that are most present for you in your home.

3. Take a few moments and consider the following questions:

   ❧ *What could your anger be telling you about what you perceive to be "wrongs" in your life?*

   ❧ *What does your worry reveal about your trust in God?*

   ❧ *What do your emotions reveal about what you think you "need?"*

4. Begin this series by humbly asking God to prepare your heart and open your eyes to areas you need to turn over to His love and wisdom.

Day 2

The Quiet Side of Crabby (one Mom's perspective)
by Daniele at Domestic Serenity

I'm not a yeller or a screamer as a Mom, thankfully it's not been an issue so far. But, I do struggle with a problem when I'm really stressed or upset. An issue that's quite opposite of raising my voice.

The stress doesn't exactly have to relate to the kids, or with feeling overwhelmed by their needs.

Sometimes my children are actually behaving, getting along, and generally not causing a fuss.

There are moments of peace in our home—imagine that!

But if this Mama is wrestling through an issue, feeling overly anxious inside *(such as when my husband lost his job),* or needing space to think or process...

I prefer to have my surroundings ultra quiet and super still.

Okay, that's putting it a bit lightly. I sometimes want all children to play the 'be seen and not heard' card, to make myself a cup of tea, and to then simply retreat from all my mothering, homemaking, housekeeping responsibilities of the day!

Somehow, the fact that I'm homeschooling four children, need to provide the family with meals, and wash our laundry doesn't compute in those moments. This self-focused vision grows overly large, and I serve my needs alone before my children or my home.

You see, for some moms, our struggle may not come out in loud, angry words or unintentional yelling across the room. Maybe you're more like me, and find that the peace and quiet you really do require in order to feel refreshed, becomes an itty-bitty idol demonstrated by a self-serving attitude.

Until it's no longer itty-bitty, right?

First, allow me to encourage you to carve out the slice of serenity you need in your days—for processing, for prayer, for focus. It's true...the quiet and silence does refresh you, so take it where possible. Make it priority.

Where the supernatural help of God's Spirit needs to flow is often the same place I find myself—you'll eventually need to release the quiet and engage in the busy, rumbly-tumbly loudness of childhood and motherhood.

You'll need to fully give yourself over to loving your children, training them, and making memories with them...even while you're thinking things through and feeling strained.

It's hard to adopt this attitude when stressed—I know. That's why we need God's help.

But, we didn't take on mothering or staying home with our children so they can primarily 'play quietly in their rooms', did we? No, not at all.

TODAY—seek God's assistance, ask for His presence to sustain you in the noise, just as He does in the quiet. He's already available... just ask.

Response

1. In what ways do you relate to Daniele and what she says in this passage? Are you a loud mama, do you struggle with needing peace and quiet, or a little of both?

2. Take a moment and read Philippians 4:4-8. How does knowing that the "Lord is near" make a difference in our anxiety? What is the promise of this passage?

3. When are some times in your day when you can carve out those quiet moments just for you?

4. What are some refreshing things you can do? (eat a special treat, read a book, watch a favorite TV show, catnap)

Let us *not*

become weary

in doing *good*

for at the proper time
we will reap a *harvest*

IF WE DO NOT

give up

Galatians 6:9 [NIV]

Day 3

10 Ways To Create a Home of Warmth and Grace

by Denise at Little House on the Valley

We've all heard the familiar phrases:

If mama ain't happy, ain't nobody happy

and

Happy wife, happy life.

Even though we throw those words around in a fun light-hearted way, there couldn't be more truth hidden beneath them. We as moms hold an honored position of making or breaking the mood of anger, discontent, and crabbiness in our homes.

Maybe you have found yourself like me, getting short-tempered with my kids when I wish I could have held my tongue or shown more grace in the heat of the moment?

There can be so many reasons that we as moms end up acting out of our Adam nature and not with a softened, spirit-filled heart. For me it is a daily journey to keep seeking the Lord and examining ways I can prepare my home, my children, and myself for a good day. We, as keepers of our dwellings, have the power to set our home's thermometer in both practical and spiritual ways.

When I have bad days or stress-filled moments, I realize the degrees of joy, peace, and calmness in my home are a direct measure of my own physical, spiritual and mental well-being.

Over the last year, I have been making some intentional changes to help me set a different tone to our home and cultivate more warmth and grace in the atmosphere. Here are 10 ways I found that help me to combat the anxiety and anger that can arise in my home.

10 Ways To Create A Home of Warmth and Grace

1. Get Rest. I still stay up late sometimes so I have time with no one asking me to do anything at all. It is a sacred quiet time for me. Scheduled bedtimes for my kids and myself gives me time to stay up beyond them and still get enough sleep. I see a direct link to whether I get enough sleep and how I handle my kids the next day. If you have babies and can't control your sleep patterns, then give yourself grace and do the best you can. We have all been there and we're cheering you on!

2. Time with God. Spending time talking to God in prayer and reading the Bible has a strong impact on me as a mom. Maybe you are in a busy season and taking devotional time is next to impossible. Do what you can, when you can. I wrote a post about the struggle I was having in this area, you can read the post below, where I started *giving up perfect hours for divine minutes*. I hope that post will encourage you to grab a few minutes here or there. Staying in the presence of God gives me strength to be proactive rather than reactive when anger arises in our home.

3. Simplify Schedules. We limit outside activities,or at least try to have seasons of off time to keep stress levels lower. I have learned to allow margin for rest, for fun, and just being together. I can tend to be task oriented. When I spend direct one on one time with my kids, (Not just homeschooling them) playing a game, looking them in the eye and giving them my attention, the level of anger in my kids comes down considerably and we feel better.

4. Clutter Busting. Keeping a few most important areas of my home de-cluttered keeps me less stressed and less angry. Not perfect but picked up through the day. I am also trying to train my kids to pick up after themselves. This is a hard area for us, but we keep working on it, and as we do it seems to bring a peace and a whole lot less anxiety for us all.

5. Give up Perfection. The only one perfect is God. I am reminded of this when I put expectations that are too high on myself. There is nothing that gets me more angry inside and lashing out then the pressure I put on myself to do too much. When we can let go of striving for perfect, we can rest in grace and let God work on our hearts. This softens us to be better moms and wives.

6. Meal Plan. When I know what is for dinner first thing in the morning this makes the day go better. Just planning it out is a simple thing to do, but sometimes I forget, and then I end up in a panic to get dinner made in time. I love my crockpot for ease and anything I can do to make meal times smooth in the evening really helps all of us stay sane. The meal planning guides provided here on The Better Mom are a great place to start.

7. Schedule Mom Time Out. Time outs are crucial for me to regroup and feel human. I encourage you to take time outs through the day. Try to simply go to your bedroom for five minutes and breathe—this does wonders for us as moms. If your kids take naps, then you have some time to soak in the silence. Doing anything here or there for yourself is so important in refueling and rejuvenating. A date with your husband, reading a good book, any hobby or interest that is just for you is important to feed your soul and make you a calmer mother.

8. Play Music. I play music every day in our home, and it works like magic. My kids might be fighting a lot or I might need to cool down too. Music works so well to change the atmosphere of our home or to keep it peaceful.

9. Give Grace for Limitations. We are women with hormone changes going on all the time. Hormones are a normal part of our ever-changing bodies, but it's good to recognize them as a valid mood changer. Communicating with our kids and husbands when we don't feel well is a good idea. Recognizing any medical limitations gives everyone in our home room to extend grace to each other.

10. Scripture Memory. Memorizing scriptures as a family, with my kids, and for myself has made such a difference in our home. When situations come up where we get angry, I can turn to the scriptures we have learned and get my kids to recite them back to me, or I recite them as a reminder when things are not going well. There is nothing that works better in the heat of the moment then saying out loud, "I can do all things through Christ who strengthens me"! I encourage you to memorize scriptures with your kids and for yourself.

I hope these 10 ways to create a home of warmth and grace will be a guide for setting the optimal temperature in your home. We as moms don't have to have it all figured out, but together we can walk day by day to create a home that reflects Christ.

1. What one of Denise's ten ways can you implement today? List specific steps you will take to make this happen.

2. What are you already doing to make your home a home of warmth and grace?

3. Take a moment and read Matthew 5:14-16. How do Jesus' words apply to your role as a mom in the home? In ways can you be a light in your home?

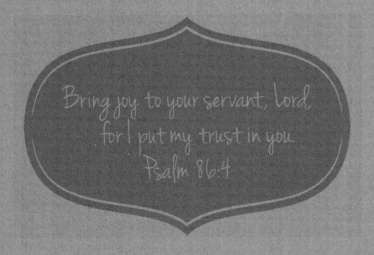

Bring joy to your servant, Lord,
for I put my trust in you.
Psalm 86:4

Day 4

4 Steps To Tame Red-Faced Mama Anger
by Christy at One Fun Mom

I've been angry.

I've been angry about broken dishes.

I've been angry over noisy kids.

I've been angry over incessant bickering in the car.

I've been angry.

I'm not proud of it, but I want you to know that if you've yelled or fumed or slammed or maybe spanked too hard...you're not alone. My cheeks flush to admit it, but I've been angry.

What can us mamas who battle real anger do?

Five years ago I was called to the table on my anger. I knew I struggled. I knew the guilt of sitting by my children's beds at night crying and praying for change.

Crying and praying only get us so far.

We need to act if things are out of control.

I started seeking out resources. I prayed about finding a counselor we could afford. I began attending a (free) ministry called *Celebrate Recovery*.

And I fell at the feet of Jesus. The very first step for me was casting everything I had been carrying on Him.

- 🙢 *Finances*
- 🙢 *Children's behavior*
- 🙢 *Marriage*
- 🙢 *Household duties*
- 🙢 *Schedule*
- 🙢 *Outside relationships*
- 🙢 *Past hurts*
- 🙢 *Family dynamics.*
- 🙢 *Children's personalities*
- 🙢 *My inadequacies*
- 🙢 *Work*

These are all factors that can play into our anger.

Likewise, if we have hurts and habits that we have not dealt with, those can manifest in anger. If you really struggle with anger, here are a few steps to take right now.

1. Let go. Let go of the denial. Denial won't heal you. Let go of the hiding. Satan lives in dark places and tells us lies when we insist on hiding. Let go of "tomorrow I will change." Change today. Let go of blame. No matter how awful we may think our children are, or how terribly we've been treated by others, or how badly our life is going—acting out of anger is our fault and we need to deal with it.

2. Realize anger itself isn't wrong. No, it's not wrong to feel angry. God gave us our emotions and feelings and it's not wrong to experience them. What is wrong is acting out in anger—yelling, screaming, hurting, hitting, throwing, even talking with that super irritated tone in our voice. We need to learn to experience our anger without hurting others (or ourselves).

3. Find one help today. The first thing I did was start looking online. Some of the following are affiliate links for books and CDs I listened to.

- *Freedom From The Spirit of Anger* (this is a free podcast and was very helpful for me).
- *Becoming Emotionally Whole* by Charles Stanley.
- *The Anger Workbook for Christian Parents* by Les Carter and Frank Minrith.
- *Life's Healing Choices: Freedom from Your Hurts, Hang-ups, and Habits* by John Baker. This book helps us start to deal with and heal from our past.
- *She's Gonna Blow!: Real Help for Moms Dealing with Anger* by Julie Ann Barnhill

4. Seriously, start praying and seeking help. I mention I found myself at a Celebrate Recovery meeting. I was scared and nervous and honestly didn't even realize I was there for me. I thought I was helping out someone else. When I got there and everyone was broken and genuine and seeking God without their Sunday masks on I was hooked. It felt like real church.

Maybe Celebrate Recovery (CR) isn't for you. I've heard that Beth Moore has a great study called *Breaking Free* that goes through a lot of similar things to CR. Or maybe you can form a group with other moms and go through the Anger Workbook mentioned above. Perhaps you will call your church and the perfect counselor or pastor will be available to meet with you.

Just do something. Make a move to start working through the anger. Today.

I will be the first to say that I don't have this all figured out. As I write this I think I should probably go back and start re-reading some of these books again. I'm okay with that. I know that I've made amazing progress from five years ago. I am not perfect. At stressful times, anger and patience can be a bigger struggle than at other times—but I continue to seek healing and Jesus.

Come to me, all you who are weary and burdened, and I will give you rest. Take my yoke upon you and learn from me, for I am gentle and humble in heart, and you will find rest for your souls. For my yoke is easy and my burden is light. Matthew 11:28-30

Response

1. Take a few minutes and read Exodus 15:22-27. In verse 26, how does God reveal himself? In other words, what is the name he uses of himself?

2. Sometimes when life is hard, God is really trying to heal us. The healing God wanted to do in his people was in their hearts. What areas of your heart need the most healing? Is it something from your past? Sinful habits?

3. Fear and shame often keep us from reaching out to others to help. Are there people you need to reach out to either begin, or continue, on the path of healing?

4. Have you found yourself acting in anger?

5. Which of the items in the list above do you think play into your anger? How can you begin to work through one of those items?

Be Careful Momma Mouth What You Say

by Carlie Kercheval at Today's Frugal Mom

How many of you remember the lyrics of the children's song, "O Be Careful?" It is a sweet song that many of us have learned over the years. Whether in Sunday school or at home, this song is a classic amongst many Christian families. While this song is meant for young children, it is a song that can teach us many things as adults as well. When I learned this song as a child at church one Sunday with my Great-Grandmother, little did I know that God would use it to convict me of my sin some 20 years later—as an adult.

This song teaches many different lessons about the importance of being careful with our eyes, hands, ears, and feet. However, it was particularly the last verse of this song that God used to begin to show me the importance of getting my anger under control, specifically related to the words that I spoke to my children.

The last verse of the song says...

> *O be careful little mouth what you say*
> *O be careful little mouth what you say*
> *There's a Father up above*

And He's looking down in love
So, be careful little mouth what you say

Are you being careful momma mouth what you say? Or are you allowing your anger to get the best of you when frustration sets in toward your children? I, for one, have been guilty more times than I care to admit with speaking unkind words out of this momma mouth. But thankfully for you and I, there is forgiveness and mercy at the feet of Jesus. I want to share with you a couple of ways that God has taken me from defeat to victory in this area of my life. Perfect? No. Better? Yes. I am confident that if you stop to do these simple things and not give up, you too, sweet momma mouth, will find victory in Christ Jesus!

Simple Ways to Keep Your Momma Mouth in Check

1. **Be Honest About.** It This is simple enough right? Yes, it really is. When you mess up with your momma mouth, be honest and forthcoming about it. Be honest with your children that you said something that is not pleasing to God. Be honest with your spouse that you need help in this area. Be honest with your God and confess your sin because He is faithful and just to forgive (1 John 1:9 KJV). Depending on the severity of your anger, it is also wise to seek accountability from a Pastor or biblical counselor.

2. **Create A Confession List.** This simple step alone has changed my life. When God first gave my husband and I the vision for our *Learning to Speak Life* ministry—it was birthed out of a confession list my husband and I were creating for our marriage. We prayerfully searched through the scriptures to find verses that pertained specifically to *building a Christ-centered marriage*. I took this very same principle and applied it to my mouth. And it has been life changing.

3. Pray And Read Your Bible. This goes without saying. By having constant conversation with God through prayer and putting your eyes upon His word, you will begin to realize that we are not to condemn ourselves for our sin and through His power we can be changed. Never doubt God's ability to work through your life. All you have to do is be willing to say YES to His will. He will show you what you need to do in your own personal situation to enable you to begin to speak His life-giving words in place of angry words that hurt your children.

4. Don't Give Up. I'd venture to say that this is one of the most important parts of our journey to overcome speaking harsh words out of anger. But God's word is true. If we will apply the principles we learn, He promises us that He is faithful to perform His word (1 Thessalonians 5:24 KJV).

Hang in there sweet momma, you can overcome this area of your life. If you will faithfully begin to apply the steps above and not give up, you will establish a strong habit in your life that will transform a generation, believe me, I know. Rest assured that you can do this with God's help! I'll be praying for you every step of the way!

Response

1. Take a moment and read James 3:3-12. What does James compare the tongue to?

2. How would you summarize the warning in this passage from James?

3. Jesus taught that we speak out of the condition of our heart. How would someone describe the condition of your heart based on the content of your speech?

4. Do you find yourself making excuses for how you speak to your children?

5. Which of the steps above can you start adapting?

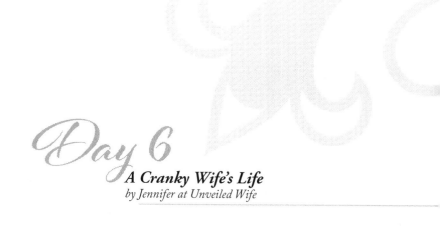

Day 6

A Cranky Wife's Life
by Jennifer at Unveiled Wife

A cranky wife cannot enjoy her day. Her insides feel twisted as her mind has a difficult time processing anything except lamenting, "Why me?" She is quick to get angry and even quicker at responding to her husband or children without thoughtfulness or patience.

Her face remains crinkled up as if disgusted at the way the day is going. Agitation and irritation sit on either shoulder convincing her of why she should snap back to her loved ones with a lack of kindness that is sure to drive away any inconveniences. A cranky wife pursues self-preservation. Her posture and her body language reveal her attitude and outlook on life. She lacks peace and her heart longs for rest.

A cranky wife loses intimacy with her husband.

I know because I have been a cranky wife. I have seen my husband's face turn curious as he looks upon his bride who morphed from pleasant to nagging, peaceful to raging, content to disappointed, loving to unkind...wondering to himself, what happened?

The cranky can last only a few seconds or it can trickle into days, months, years. Why?

Why do we let cranky be OK?

I have allowed my heart to justify why I can let "cranky" come out and rule my life. In those moments of weakness, I hurt my husband. I fail to communicate in a gentle way and I hurt my husband. In an effort to reconcile, yet still affected by my attitude I say, "Sorry, I am just cranky." (Not really an apology, but more of a justification for my right to act however I want, disregarding those around me.) It hurts my husband.

How can we as wives resolve to not be cranky?

It is a choice of surrendering your flesh. In those moments where cranky wants to come out and expose how you feel, you have a choice to lay down your justifications, take a deep breath, and ask God to help you be better.

I acknowledge this has been a difficult challenge for me as a wife. *I easily let my circumstances dictate how I feel.* But in my heart I know I have a choice. I can choose to be better. My marriage will suffer if I don't. I resolve to take a breath in those moments my flesh feels weak. I resolve to think through my attitudes and actions before lashing out. And I know that with God's help I can change this part of my character and be a wife who does not allow cranky to rule.

Will you join me?

1. Do you think there is ever a time when it's okay to be cranky?

2. Do you notice your crankiness hurting those around you?

3. Have you ever been hurt by someone else's crankiness?

You turned my wailing into *dancing*;
you removed my sackcloth and
clothed me with joy,
that my heart may sing your praises
and not be silent.
Lord my God, I will *praise you forever.*
Psalm 30:11-12

Idols Of A Mom's Heart
by Ruth Simons at Gracelaced

*"What makes us crabby often reveals
where our idols dwell."
~Ruth Chou Simons*

The reasons, factors, conditions, and circumstances are endless. There is always an excuse for why I can justify my waking up on the proverbial wrong side of the bed:

"It makes me crazy when I wake up to children screaming."

"I just need everyone to be quiet."

"I'm so annoyed by the kids' whining."

"Why isn't anyone else doing their job (like I am)."

Mom's frustrated, tired, cranky, and annoyed...again.

And while no one will argue that motherhood is very often exhausting and stretching in every way, the reality of the cranky mom syndrome is that our attitudes as moms have less to do with how our households are functioning, and more about the function of expectations in our homes. My daily life as a mom is replete with examples of how I often turn training into expectations, expectations into idols:

- The desire to wake up to a quiet house is reasonable, but has it squelched my ability to respond to my children's (sometimes foolish) needs with patience?
- Is my need for peace and quiet so strong I'm willing to be unkind in the pursuing of it?
- Does my children's whining annoy and inconvenience me more than it drives me to pray and train? Am I so prideful in the way I perceive my diligence that I am blind to teachable moments?

One of my favorite authors, Elyse Fitzpatrick, says this from her book, *Idols Of The Heart*:

> *If you're willing to sin to obtain your goal or if you sin when you don't get what you want, then your desire has taken God's place and you're functioning as an idolater.*

The starting point for us in any difficult parenting situation, in any challenging schedule, in any wearisome trial, is to examine what idols our attitudes and actions are pointing to. You see, my intolerance, impatience, frustration, and crabbiness, can often be traced back to an inordinate desire for ease, comfort, calm, and self-assurance.

What makes us crabby often reveals where our idols dwell.

My idolatry of those things make me willing to act in whatever way seems fitting when something (or someone) stands in the way of that ease, comfort, calm, and self-assurance. Can you see it in your own life?

Replace Idolatry With The Worship Of Christ

Friends, our only hope for overcoming the idols in our lives is to *replace them* with He who is greater. There is no magic formula or instant solution to overcoming a bad attitude or a crabby outlook... but there is hope when we know where true hope may be found. When we worship Jesus, and focus our hearts on who he is and what he has accomplished on the Cross, we begin to worship Him, and not our comfort. We begin to see Him, and not our expectations, as being worthy of worship. We begin to trust in his work in us, rather than our work for him.

Response

1. Take a moment and read Exodus 20:3. How would you summarize this verse in your own words?

2. In our sinfulness, we can exchange the worship of our Creator for some part of creation. This might be comfort, pleasure, rest, time, etc. Anything we desire more than God can become a false god or idol if we're not careful. Why is this so dangerous?

3. Is there something that consistently makes me crabby? What idol does that crabbiness indicate?

4. What comfort do I crave as a mother? Do I find myself caving into that craving and becoming cranky when that comfort seems far away?

Come, all you who are thirsty,
come to the waters;
and you who have no money,
come, buy and eat!
Come, buy wine and milk without
money and without cost.
Isaiah 55:1

1 Root of Anger and 3 Ways to Control It

by Christin at Joyful Mothering

Do not be conformed to a lifestyle of anger.
Discover its root so it can be controlled.

Anger is triggered by many factors, and sometimes one person can carry more of those triggers than others.

Some of us have deep wells of hurt, regret, or fear that can transform into anger at a moment's notice.

I had one such incident the day after Christmas with my eleven year old daughter.

She displayed some behavior that I've noticed in myself that I'm not particularly fond of and I reacted. (With more bad behavior, go figure). This created a reaction in my daughter and things escalated quickly. Before long I realized what had happened and after unloading loud words and punishments, I began to recognize what I had done.

Most of us have flaws that we'd rather not see birth out of our children. Beyond that, recognizing where the origin of our anger or frustration lies is the key to eliminating much of that anger. Rather than laboring to control our anger, perhaps it's a good idea if we face it head on.

The Root of Anger

How can we get to the root of what's making us angry and deal with it? While we'll need to train our reactions in the short run, sometimes working through root anger issues can take years to sort out and heal from. This may take some time to reflect, perhaps journal, and really dig deep.

Sometimes it really requires some searching to finally reach the problem. Aside from part of my frustrations stemming from fear that my children will pick up my bad habits, I have several other anger issues stemming from selfishness, unrealistic expectations, and feeling overwhelmed that can all trigger reactive responses.

Consequences

Anger in and of itself is not a sin in some cases (it really depends on your heart). However, responding in anger can be and it carries consequences with it. We can wound our children in our anger. We can break their spirits or even be a root cause of anger in their own lives. I don't think it is something we should brush off as normal or no big deal. It is something that we should be *taking diligent steps to minimize and control.*

But how?

First, begin with prayer. Ask for God to change your heart because it's really the molding of the Holy Spirit that is going to be effective in our change.

Second, be willing to be molded. We can't expect change when we don't want to be changed. It's going to take some effort on our part, not merely a change made up in our minds, but some purging of our heart. I think we expect that anger will be lifted from our lives with little to no effort, but that's just not the case. It really does require some chiseling and pain to purge those areas.

Third, memorize scripture dealing with anger and the tongue. This simple task can be very helpful in the midst of an episode rising in us. If we can stop our anger from elevating from a frustration to an explosion, we'll begin to learn self-control.

One way to do this is to be familiar with verses on anger so they can be brought to memory when we feel those frustrations rising in us. James 1:19 and Proverbs 15:1 are great places to start.

None of these are meant to be a cure-all for all anger issues. They are merely a starting point, and we all need to start somewhere. It begins with recognizing we have anger, pinpointing it's root, and taking steps to control it.

Response

1. What's one thing you have found that helps you deal with anger?

2. Am I willing to recognize that I struggle with anger? In what ways do I struggle with anger? (list specific occurrences, or something that angers you consistently.)

3. Take a moment and read Proverbs 15:1. How does a "gentle answer" turn away wrath or anger?

4. What are specific examples of gentleness in parenting? What about gentleness in marriage?

When the Load of Worry
Makes You Angry
by Jessica Smartt at "Smartter" Each Day

During my seventh grade year, my English teacher went through a divorce.

As the year went on, it was obvious how stressed and burdened she was. Her eyes had thick bags underneath. She rarely wore makeup, and gained a bunch of weight. She'd usually arrive flustered, papers thick and crumpled, graded late and harsh.

She'd perk up reading *The Diary of Anne Frank*, but would get provoked by the slightest disruption. You could feel the tension, feel the anger.

You know, I hate "taking things out on my kids." I'm better than that—I should be, anyway. Yet I still do it.

Motherhood is a race, long and sweaty. It takes muscle, concentration, and full-bent focus. It takes everything you have, even on a good day.

And the bad days? I've found it's nearly impossible to do it well when I'm labored down with extra loads.

My baggage? *Mine is worry*. Oh, I worry.

I daily carry around fears for my son's health. *His life-threatening allergies and asthma* can feel too big to carry.

I worry for our finances, tension creeping in with each purchase, each stacking pile of bills.

When it gets really bad, I worry about my worry.

I'll never be a good enough mom. I shouldn't have more children, or home school...Worry freezes me in an oppressive prison of self-doubt and condemnation.

I carry these thoughts and fears, and in the meantime I wipe bottoms, and read Corduroy, and pry older brother off younger during a wrestling match-turned-taunting.

And if I don't watch it, I start feeling like Mrs. E., the seventh-grade English teacher. I'm snapping at people, sometimes even (gulp) screaming...My voice gets unnecessarily loud, my feelings unnecessarily hurt.

I'm burdened, and I get angry too easily.

Is there a cure? There is! Praise the Lord;
He doesn't leave us in this mess.

Come to me, He says, all you who are weary, and burdened, and I will give you rest...Casting all your anxieties on Him, because He cares for you. (Matthew & I Peter...)

So what does this look like, in real life, in a house with a grumpy mom and little ones who yell at the dinner table? I'll show you, exactly.

Today, I'm pregnant. First trimester, dry heaving, bone tired, napping-more-than-the-kids kind of pregnant.

Friends, I've been a pathetic mom. Dinners are boxed or take-out (this from an organic girl), laundry in mounds, Bible verses unsaid, rooms uncleaned...I'm embarrassed and worried at my failures, and I carry it around.

When I find myself angry, I could get depressed and pout...or I could come.

Lord Jesus, I'm worried. I feel like I have nothing to give my family. I'm afraid I'm not doing enough. I feel like I'm doing an awful job at this. Take this weight. I give you all that I have—help me. Help me be a mom today.

And then I know what you know, too—that the peace that passes understanding is a real thing. And that He is the lifter of my loads, and the giver of my peace. It's really, really true.

Response

1. Do you carry the burden of worry?

2. Does it affect the way you parent?

3. Jesus has a lot to say about worry. Take a few minutes and read Matthew 6:25-34. What does worry reveal about our confidence in God?

4. In what ways can worry about tomorrow rob us of joy for today?

10 Ways To Create a Home of Warmth & Grace

1. Get rest
2. Spend time with God
3. Simplify my schedule
4. De-clutter: keep at least some areas of my home tidy
5. Give up perfection
6. Meal plan
7. Mom time out
8. Play music
9. Give grace to myself and others
10. Scripture memory

Day 10

Cultivating Joy Through a Simpler Life
by Cassandra at The Unplugged Family

Joy is found in the simple life.
Embrace quieter days, hold on to peace.

Ask another Mom how she's doing and the most common answer is: "I'm just SO busy!".

We live in a culture that tells us the more activities our children are involved with, the more successful they will be when they grow to be adults. And it seems millions of parents are buying the lie.

So many Moms (and Dads!) are doing far more than caring for a family. Family life looks starkly different than it has for the majority of history. We've come to a place where we feel we can never do enough 'stuff.' Life itself can already seem like a blur of everyday responsibilities: cleaning, doing laundry, cooking, grocery shopping, homeschooling or helping with homework, playing with the children, etc.

Beyond that, most families are running an additional weekly marathon of playdates with friends, church services, multiple church activities, countless extracurricular activities, and an endless reel of sports involvement. Every night feels like a checklist of unending tasks and commitments and every weekend is a whirlwind of running here, there, and everywhere.

It's no wonder exhaustion takes over. It's no wonder stress is the overriding emotion for so many Moms. It's no wonder millions of Moms are 'grouchy' and unable to find peace in their calling.

A hyperactive lifestyle robs us of our joy.

If we are always running, running, running, when do we rest? When do we reflect on what matters? When do we spend time around the table praying and seeking God? When do we just curl up and read together, or gaze out the window and talk of nature's beauty in the wintry frost?

When can we just breathe?

More is not better, in fact, more is almost always worse. The busier our children are, the less time they have to focus on the most important things—God, family, people, relationships, learning for themselves, and service.

When we set the example of a slower, simpler life, we are teaching our children how to seek joy in simplicity.

I believe the only way we can truly center ourselves and focus on what really matters is to slow down. I'm not suggesting laziness, I'm suggesting intentional simplicity. Simplicity can still be active and busy (and it will be if you're a Mom!) but it is minimal. We minimize what doesn't really matter to maximize what really DOES.

As moms we need to slow down and set the example for our entire family. An overscheduled, busy, hectic lifestyle is one void of peace because the Prince of Peace has no place in our day. Or our week. Maybe even our year.

God doesn't call us to live a busy life. He calls us to live a purposeful life. But not our purposes—His purposes.

And when we walk alongside Him, we are forced to slow down, reflect, serve, and humble ourselves. It is there we find the deepest joy and overflowing peace for ourselves and our children.

Be blessed in the simple things today, Mom!

Response

1. Is there any activity or ministry I can eliminate to make my days more purposeful?

2. What about for each child? For our family?

3. What is an activity we can do when we have down time to seize the moment?

4. Read Mark 2:23-27. The Sabbath in Jesus' day, and for many Jewish people today, was a day of rest. It was a time to cease from the normal hustle and bustle of life. It was carving out time to cease from work and trusting that God had things under control. How can you, or your family, implement the Sabbath principle in your busy life?

May the God of hope fill you with all
joy and peace as you trust in him,
so that you may *overflow with hope* by the
power of the Holy Spirit.
Romans 15:13

Day 11

How to Restore Your Soul When You Feel Like You're Losing Your Mind
by Lisa Jacobson at Club31 Women

To this day I don't know just how it happened.

She was the most adorable baby girl you've ever seen and I was beside myself with gratefulness for her.

First there was her big brother who was very busy and all of 18 months old. Then there was this tiny pink thing. My very own sweetheart.

She was beautiful alright, but not the greatest sleeper. She wanted to nurse all night long and it took some of the fun out of it, if you know what I mean?

So I'd been doing this all night party thing for several weeks when I started getting delirious. A little loco. One night I found myself walking with her in circles until 2 am when finally...at last...I got the baby darling to sleep. I gently tucked her in bed and quietly crawled in next to my sound out husband.

And collapsed into a deep sleep.

For about 12 whole minutes.

That's when I heard her soft cries starting up again. I roused myself and leaned over the white, lacey crib and I...well, I screamed. Something like this: Ahhhhhhhhhhhh!!

My poor husband bolted upright in bed, immediately on high alert. "What is going on here?!"

I stared at him wide eyed—nearly as shocked as he was. Disbelief at what I'd done. Ashamed and embarrassed.

"I dunno, Honey. I guess I kinda...snapped."

And so her daddy tenderly picked up our baby doll and took over where I left off. But as he left the room, he gently admonished,

"Hey, don't let yourself get in that place again, okay?"

Ah yes, That Place.

I can assure you that I never intended to "get there".

Since then—four boys and four girls later—I've been learning *how to avoid getting to That Place.*

Here are a few tips on how to restore your soul when you feel like you're losing your mind.

A mix of spiritual, physical, and just plain practical ways to keep from yelling into the baby's crib and other crazy mama moments:

1. ***Get the rest you require.*** Make it a high priority because it can make all the difference. Sleep deprivation is a terrible thing. Go to bed early or take a nap. Ask friends or family to take over and curl up in a quiet place. Get serious about getting some sleep.

2. ***Do this in Christ's strength.*** Not your own. Don't convince yourselfthat "I" can do this, but minister in His power rather than your own. Place Bible verses around the house, sing praises, and pray as you go throughout your day. Motherhood is a spiritual endeavor.

3. ***Don't neglect your own needs.*** Sometimes a mom gets so busy she forgets to eat right, to shower, and even go to the bathroom. She forgets to love with her husband or talk to a good friend. My dear, how can you fill up your child's heart if yours is on empty?

4. Be willing to ask for help. At first it felt rather stupid and weak, but I figured it was better than a break down. So one older lady folded clothes for me. Another teen girl came over to play with the children. We even sacrificed for a season and had a cleaning lady come in.

It's been 18 years since I yelled into the crib. That baby girl is now a lovely young lady and I asked if she remembered me losing it with her. She put her arms around me and said she only remembers snuggling together, reading stories aloud, and splashing in mud puddles.

And I'm beside myself with gratefulness. My very own sweetheart.

1. What kinds of things do you do to *restore your soul*?

2. Have you had any yelling into the crib moments?

3. Read Mark 1:35-37. What does Jesus do to refresh?

4. Where does he go?

5. When does he go?

6. What do you learn most about Jesus' example?

What Every Weary Mom
Needs to Know

{four tips for when it gets tough}

1. Steal moments with God.

2. Lean into the work.

3. Find an encouraging friend.

4. Embrace the motherhood mission.

Day 12

Reasons Why Your Child Needs to See Your Anger (And Truths They can Learn from It)

by Tricia Goyer at TriciaGoyer.com

We work so hard NOT to be angry as moms, but there is a time we need to show our anger: to benefit our kids.

Reasons why your child needs to see your anger:

- ❧ My child needs to know that some things are unacceptable, such as lying, stealing, or unkind words.
- ❧ My child needs to know he/she will be defended. My husband often says, "Do not hit my little girl like that," or "Do not push my little boy."
- ❧ My child needs to see we care about injustice in the world. It's OK to get angry about child abuse or deception and let our kids see it.

If you do get angry:

- ❧ Make sure it's justified. Do you have a good reason?

- 🙠 *Make sure it's controlled.* Using a firm voice with your child is OK. Yelling or using physical outbursts is not.
- 🙠 Let your child know that Jesus got angry too. He was angry with those who believed they were too good to need him. He was angry at those who used God's house to make money and cheat others.
- 🙠 Brainstorm IF there is something you can do about injustice. Can you raise money for an organization who is fighting against an unjust cause?

After you get angry, turn to prayer.

- 🙠 Pray with the child who committed the offense, seeking God's forgiveness.
- 🙠 Pray with the child who was offended.
- 🙠 Pray about injustice.
- 🙠 Pray for compassion.
- 🙠 Pray that God will give you His heart for the hurting.
- 🙠 Pray for those who are walking in sin and hurting others.

What your child will learn:

- 🙠 That everyone makes mistakes.
- 🙠 That *God is willing to forgive.*
- 🙠 That there are many people who need our prayers.
- 🙠 That we can learn from our mistakes and the mistakes of others.
- 🙠 That we can be angry and maintain control. As Proverbs 29:11 says, *"A fool gives full vent to his anger, but a wise man keeps himself under control."* (NIV)

Final things to be emphasized:

- 🙠 Anger is a temptation.
- 🙠 What we do after *getting angry can lead to a sin*...or it can lead to a positive change.

- God doesn't want us to vent our anger.
- We need to make sure that what we're getting mad about is justified.
- Pray and ask God what He wants you to do with your feelings.

Response

1. What do you think? How has getting angry benefited your kids?

2. Do you think it is ever OK to show anger?

3. In the Bible, we are told that God gets angry. His anger is really an expression of what he loves. So when God gets angry at deceit, it reveals his love for truth. When God gets angry at immorality, it reveals God's love for purity. When God gets anger at oppression, it reveals his love for justice. Unlike us, God's anger is always justified because of his holiness.

4. What does your anger say about what you love?

5. Unlike God's anger, how does your anger sometimes reveal selfishness?

Make a careful exploration of *who you are* and
the work you have been given,
and then sink yourself into that.

∽ Don't be impressed with yourself ∽

Don't compare yourself with others. Each of you
must **take responsibility** for doing the creative
best you can with your own life.

Galatians 6:4-5 NLT

Day 13

The Grace I Need. Why Do I Run From It?

by Natalie Falls at NatalieFalls.com

This last weekend would have been easy to ignore. I could pretend it didn't happen. Pretend my blood didn't boil with frustration towards my son. I could pretend that the kink in my neck is from how I slept wrong, instead of admitting that my muscles tightened from my anger. I could pretend. I could push guilt and conviction under a pretty rug. My pretty pride rug. Whatever you do, don't lift it up!

And that's exactly what I did, I shoved it under that rug and I tried my hardest to forget about it.

I didn't want to take the time to deal with myself.

I didn't want to feel my pride crushed. I wasn't in the mood to be humbled. Some days I just want a break. I want to be a mom that has it all together and doesn't have to do any work to be awesome. Some days I want to run away from the pain of my flesh. I want to ignore the help and grace that can change me. I want to do it on my own.

And then I break. I can only run for so long. Ignore. Hide. But my rug can only hide so much.

My son's soft green eyes look up at me and his words are tender. "It's okay mom, nobody's perfect. I'm not even perfect!" And then he wanted to make me happy again. "Did you know mom, when we go to heaven there will be no more sin or sadness, and we will all be perfect. AND...there will be wrestling! There will be wrestling, right mom?" Tears fill my eyes, and I fall more in love with my son. "Of course baby, there will be wrestling."

I am thankful that God can use a five-year-old to teach me about the important things in this life. Things that I can't hide. And I am humbled once again by the grace that has been given to me.

God's grace, once again, fills me and changes me. Why do I ignore, fight, and hide? Haven't I learned yet? Grace, the precious gift I do not deserve, it's making me into the woman I long to be.

I want to be a mom that grabs hold of grace, not perfection.

Response

1. Do I struggle with attempting perfection? In what ways?

2. How have my kids taught me about God's grace?

3. Take a moment and read Ephesians 2:8-10. God our Father is pleased with us not because of our perfection, but because of Jesus' perfection. Our faith in him makes us clean, holy, and fully accepted. How can grace keep your heart from growing weary?

Day 14

Overcoming Anger With Eternity
by Kara Chupp at The Chuppies

Eternity changes everything.

I've written in the past about *why I don't want our children to feel at home here.*

Because...

I want their true home to be in Heaven.

But...

I've also come to realize that when I lose my temper and the anger rises,

And especially when I start to see a pattern of quick-to-annoyance-why-can't-they-all-just-do-what-they're-told-and-quit-dropping-full-cups-of-yogurt-on-clean-tables—it is usually because of two things:

1. **I've allowed idols to creep in.** If you missed my friend Ruth's chapter, Idols of a Mom's Heart on page 27, please take time to read it.

2. **I'm suffering from eternity amnesia.** Whether I say it or not, I'm living like Heaven isn't real. As if my current state of laundry piles, runny noses, bills, and stringy gum stuck in hair is all

there is. I have forgotten eternity and the promises of forever that I have in Christ.

"I often lived as an eternity amnesiac.

I, too, often lived with the unrealistic expectations and functional hopelessness that always results when you tell yourself that this life you have right here, right now, is all there is...

This present life is not all there is.
There is a forever on the other side of this life.
Eternity is not a mystical creation of overly spiritual people.
Forever is a reality...

Living in this present world is designed by God to produce three things in me—longing, readiness, and hope."

~Paul David Tripp, Forever (pages 12, 13, 14, 35)

So how does remembering Heaven change things?

How does it *help a mama who is about to lose it* because:

There is a popsicle stick stuck to the corner of the couch, he forgot to mention signing "us" up to bring cupcakes for the class party, there wasn't a trash bag in the garbage can when they scraped the breakfast plates, and *someone used a stamp pad to wallpaper her sister's room*?

Focusing on eternity reminds me that:

1. Life is not all about me. "I am not in the center of my world now, and I won't be then. What makes eternity wonderful is that God is restored to His rightful place at the center of all things."

2. My heart will only be satisfied when it finds its satisfaction in God. "In eternity I will no longer search horizontally for what I will only find vertically." *~Paul David Tripp, Forever (page 76)*

I lived a whole chunk of my life not really thinking much about Heaven. But then our daughter, Selah, died and I needed to focus on eternity.

And while it brought comfort as I thought about the future joy of seeing her again, learning about and thinking about Heaven did so much more than that because:

Heaven changes everything.

It shifts our dreams, our goals, our direction. It affects our pain, our sorrow, our fears. Heaven gives us hope.

Heaven moves us to invest in what will endure—Forever.

Heaven gives us courage to sacrifice for what will last—Forever.

Heaven reminds us of what is truly important.

Especially when I'm tempted, as a mama, to *unleash the flood gates of anger.*

Heaven calls me to patience as I remember the patient grace that God offers me daily.

> *When circumstances rise to levels of importance way beyond their actual importance, they exercise more control over us than they should...the resurrection of Jesus and the hope of forever give us a sense of priority and proportion.*
> *-Paul David Tripp, Forever (page 87)*

> *"Peace is found only in knowing that this world is meant to prepare us for the next and that the temporary pleasures and pains of this world are not our final address. When we live knowing that the God of grace will lift us out of this broken world and is now readying us for the world to come, we can face difficult without wanting to give up and experience pleasure without becoming addicted to it. We live with hope in our heart, eyes to the future, and hands holding this present world loosely."*
> *- Paul David Tripp, Forever (page 37)*

Heaven reminds me that this world is broken.

That I should not be surprised when I face frustrations and failures in myself or even in those I love best.

But that *there is hope* because Jesus said,

> *"And if I go and prepare a place for you, I will come again and will take you to myself, that where I am you may also be."*
> *~John 14:3*

And I want to live, to really live in such a way that when I reach Heaven I will say:

> *"I have come home at last! This is my real country! I belong here." ~C.S. Lewis, The Last Battle*

> *"Our citizenship is in Heaven, and from it we await a Savior, the Lord Jesus Christ." ~Philippians 3:20*

Practical Ideas for Renewing an Eternal Perspective:

- ᴥ Do a *Bible search* on verses that relate to Heaven and find creative ways to display them around the house.
- ᴥ Ask God to remind you of Heaven throughout the day, especially when you feel tempted to lash out in anger.
- ᴥ Read any of Randy Alcorn's books about Heaven. *Heaven for Kids* is probably our favorite.
- ᴥ Read Paul David Tripp's book, *Forever*, and Joni Eareckson Tada's book, *Heaven*.
- ᴥ Begin every morning thanking God that "we are looking forward to a new heavens and a new earth, in which righteousness dwells." ~2 Peter 3:13

> *Overcoming anger with eternity perspective*
> *makes it all worth it!*

Response

1. What was most thought provoking from today's chapter and why?

2. Take a moment and read Revelation 21:1-5. What characteristics about Heaven are most encouraging to you and why?

3. Take a moment and read Romans 8:18-25. Verse 23 says we "groan inwardly as we wait eagerly." For the Christian, there is a longing for the return of Christ. What are some practical ways you can keep a more eternal perspective in your marriage and family?

The Lord has done great things for us, and we are filled with joy.

Psalm 126:3

Day 15

Mom Sets the Tone (5 Ways to Reset Your Mood When Anger Strikes)
by Ruth Soukup at Living Well, Spending Less

Though it has been a few years, I can still remember the conversation like it was yesterday. In one of our marathon phone sessions, I poured out all my frustration to my sister:

Chuck is such a jerk! I'm so tired of feeling like I can't do anything right! And the girls are driving me absolutely crazy! No sooner do I get one mess cleaned up than they make another one. Annie still won't sleep through the night and Maggie refuses to sit on the potty and they both just won't. stop. whining. I feel so tired and crabby and angry! I just want to scream!

Although she was 3,000 miles away, her response stopped me dead in my tracks, and she may as well have slapped me across the face.

Six years older, with kids that were now in high school, she had already made it through those exasperating preschool years. She quietly said, "I know how hard it is, but you have to remember that a mom sets the tone for her household. The mood of your family will ultimately reflect your own. If you are crabby, they will be too."

My kids are a little older now, both potty trained and sleeping through the night. They pick up after themselves, at least some of the time, and I'm not quite as exhausted as I was when they were babies. While I still struggle with crabbiness far more than I would like to admit, over the years I have discovered a few surefire ways to improve my mood and my attitude when I am feeling on edge. They might just work for you too:

1. ***Play a game.*** I can honestly tell you that there is nothing I feel like doing less when I am crabby than *playing a game with my kids.* Even so, I have discovered that there is nothing that will reset my mood or snap me out of a funk quicker than a rousing game of hide-and-seek. There is just something so silly about a full grown adult trying to squeeze into a tight space! Other games that always seem to get us laughing include Spot It and Go Fish.

2. ***Clean something.*** I don't know about you but I get some of the best cleaning done when I am really ticked off! If you really feel like you might explode, why not channel all that anger into a power *Speed Cleaning* session, something that will actually make you feel a whole lot better when you are done rather than something that will make you feel a whole lot worse, like *yelling at your kids* or husband.

3. ***Breathe.*** I love yoga, if for no other reason than it has taught me the importance of learning how to breathe. The next time you feel tense, try this exercise: Close your eyes and take a long deep breath in through your nose, then exhale very slowly through your mouth. Do this ten more times, or until you have calmed down. I've also discovered that this is a great exercise to teach your kids when they are upset!

4. ***Take a timeout.*** If your kids or husband are truly driving you nuts and you feel like you might snap, do whatever necessary to *remove yourself from the situation.* Put your kids in their room for quiet time, take a hot bath or a long shower, or go for a walk around the block.

5. *Give yourself grace.* None of us are perfect. Every mom gets angry sometimes, and we all make mistakes. Acknowledge your feelings in the moment, tell yourself, "I am angry right now, and that is okay," then also *give yourself permission to let it go and to move on.*

Response

1. In what way have you noticed that you set the tone for your family?

2. Take a moment and read Romans 8:9-17. What does it mean to be led by the flesh?

3. What does it mean to be led by the Spirit?

4. We are not called to overcome sin by our own power. God enables us to walk in victory by the power of His Spirit. The Apostle Paul commands us to be "filled by the Spirit" in Ephesians 5:18. How should we practically surrender to God's Spirit in our lives?

Come to Me,
all you who labor
~ and are ~
heavy laden,
and I will give you

rest.

Matthew 11:28

Day 16

Take Back Your Emotions
By Brooke McGlothlin at M.O.B. Society

My youngest son has an amazing laugh.

Everyone who hears it smiles big and tells us the same thing, "he's incredible!" and I nod my head in agreement, because he is. The only problem is that his laugh drives me batty...well, sometimes.

Big Laughs in Small Spaces

As a raging introvert, the hardest part about raising two of *"those boys"* (the ones who are 250% boy?) is the constant "boy noise," especially when it's in small spaces.

I'm convinced that if we lived on 2+ acres of farm land in the country, their noise wouldn't be a problem. I could simply scoot them out the door after school and *let them be little boys.*

Unfortunately, we live on less than half an acre right on the outskirts of our city. We have one semi-climbable tree, and neighbors who we think like us in spite of the high decibels coming from our home—but we do not have room for our boys to run and be as loud as they'd like.

I long for this (LONG for it, I say) kind of life for my boys. I want them to run, fall, scrape their knees, build things from scratch, and learn to "rough it." And in spite of our close quarters, I do try to stoke their creative little boy fires as much as possible.

However...

My little rough and tumble boys are also fiddlers. Every week we drive almost four hours round trip to take them to violin lessons with the best instructor we can afford, because they have a gift and find great pleasure in playing this instrument. For the first hour or so of the trip, things are usually fine, but just give it enough time and the "big laugh in small spaces phenomenon," as we've come to call it, creeps out and starts to drive mama crazy.

My little guy, who others see as simply amazing, starts to sound like a hyena on crack...or at least it sounds that way to me.

I've asked, begged, threatened discipline, explained why it's so important to me as the driver that he keep it down, pulled over, driven faster, and thought seriously about never getting in another car with this kid for the rest of my life...but nothing works (obviously...he's six...I have a few more years before I can actually refuse to get in the car with him).

If it were only a matter of time spent in the car, I would probably be OK. But over time, an immediate physical and emotional response started to occur in me at the sound of his laughter whether we were in the car or not, and I found myself completely unable to tolerate his laughter on any level.

Not good.

I was so annoyed by my son's inability to control the power of his laugh, that I was punishing him for even having one.

Imagine that...punishing a child for laughing. Possibly one of my finest mothering moments. Most certainly one of the things my son will tell his wife one day to explain why he's so messed up.

Don't get me wrong, my son needs to learn how to control himself in confined areas so he doesn't drive everyone in his life crazy—we'll *keep working on that*—but his amazing laugh brought me an opportunity for growth too, and for that, I'm ever so thankful.

How to Take Back Your Emotions

In my ebook, *How to Control Your Emotions So They Don't Control You: A Mom's Guide to Overcoming*, I share another story that illustrates this immediate physical and emotional response. Maybe you can relate?

One particular day, my boys were filled with disobedience and hard hearts. As I sat in my driveway watching them play basketball like crazy men—disrespecting each other, and disrespecting our neighbor's basketball goal—I felt my emotions begin to run away. I started off embarrassed by their behavior. Then I got mad because it was what seemed like the millionth time I had asked them to obey with no apparent response. Anger moved into frustration because sometimes it just feels like nothing ever changes around here. Frustration led to feeling completely overwhelmed by my own inability to change their hearts. And finally, feeling overwhelmed moved to straight hopelessness and a desire to just. give. up. In a matter of about two minutes I went from 0 to 10 on the emoto-meter (you know, the one that measures when mama's going to snap??), and ended the day feeling like a total failure as a mom.

Clearly, I have a pattern of letting my
emotions run away from me.

Because we struggled so much to gain control of our son's amazing laugh, I couldn't even hear him be happy without wanting to explode. But just because I want to explode doesn't mean I have to. *With God's help, I can control my emotions* instead of letting them control me, and retrain myself to take delight in the laughter of my own child.

So can you.

1. The book of Psalms is perhaps the most honest and emotion-filled book of the Bible. For example, take a moment and read Psalm 55:1-8. What emotions do you see present in this psalm?

2. It has been said that your "emotions reveal you." They are like windows into your soul. Take a moment and write down what emotions you experience most often.

3. What does God's Word say about each of these emotions? In other words, what solution do the Scriptures provide?

3 Ways to Conquer the Inner Ugly
by Kate Battistelli at KateBattistelli.com

Here's the thing, if you're a mom then you're human and you're going to make mistakes. Your kids will frustrate you from time to time and you're going to get angry, crabby and irritated. It kind of goes with the territory so for goodness sake, stop beating yourself up over it!

We've all done it and we'll do it again. We live in a fallen world with fallen natures and it takes everything in us to conquer the sin that reigns deep within. But hear me, your children will survive your crabby days, I promise! And there's hope for change.

I'm a little further along in my parenting journey as my daughter is all grown now with children of her own so allow me to share my perspective. I *struggled with anger and crabbiness* too, still do to be honest. Mostly because I have a way in my head I think everything should be and when it doesn't look or behave the way I want it to, I snap. I answer harshly. I'm impatient. Because I want to control things and I want things a certain way—my way—which is rarely the way.

I can be selfish and think I have rights but the thing is, when we follow Christ we give up our right to ourselves. We tell the Lord with all sincerity, "I surrender all" until we don't and the inner ugly rears it's head. I'm learning (and believe me it takes a lifetime) to really surrender—my ways, my wants, my ego, my future, my worship, my time, my fuse, my control, my everything—to the one who alone can change me from the inside out.

The biggest thing I've learned is this:
the way you love is the way you'll live.

If you really do love the Lord with all your heart, mind, soul and strength then His love will flow out of you naturally. Not perfectly but naturally. Because, mama, *you'll never be perfect* and neither will I and it's okay.

We can totally stress over it, or we can stress over our kids being kids and being silly and disobedient and way too loud. Or, we can thank God for giving us the great honor of raising children, *building them into the men and women of God He's calling them to be.*

Moms are builders and it takes time to build a life. Doing the same things over and over, teaching the same lessons, correcting the same behavior, praying the same prayers can be exhausting. The tiny increments of hours and days turn to months and years. It takes years to build children into the men and women of God He's called them to be, the ones who will change the world. The ones willing to be His hands and feet to the lost and weary, the desperate and depressed, the weary and worn, no matter where He leads them.

Here are three things to help you get through and conquer the inner ugly:

1. **Pray whenever you can.** In the car pool line, making lunches in the morning, folding endless laundry, whenever. You don't have to rise with the dawn and have perfect silence and beautiful music and a lit candle to worship God. He knows. Do it when you can but do it because wherever you do it, He's there.

2. **Cultivate a heart of thankfulness.** When you really begin to thank Him for the lives He's entrusted to you, you'll look at them

differently. It's a long process this parenting thing. Just like a building grows one brick, one story at a time, raising a child is one day, one month, one year at a time.

3. Ask for forgiveness when you snap in anger. Kids deserve respect too and when we humble ourselves, *repent and ask them to forgive us* it models correct and Godly behavior because sin is sin, no matter what age we are.

So, to sum it up, I know you're doing a great job. Stop beating yourself up and get back to building those little lives.

Response

1. Do you have a hard time accepting that you're human and forgiving yourself when you struggle with anger?

2. Do you ask your children for forgiveness when you sin in this area? Why is this important?

3. Kate recognized one of her "triggers" for anger in this reading: wanting to control. Do you struggle with this desire?

4. Take a moment and read Ephesians 2:8-9. What does this passage say about our acceptance by God? How should God's grace, and not our performance, be an encouragement to us as moms?

Let us not become weary
in doing good, for at
the proper time we will reap a
harvest if we do not give up.
Galatians 6:9

Day 18

But What if You're Born Angry?
by Elisa at More To Be

My mom always said that I was born angry. She would tenderly tease that I was really a Viking, because from my earliest of days I had a short fuse and sharp tongue.

Of course, my teenage feelings about her perspective on my temperament was along the lines of "Whatever...it's your problem not mine!"

That was until I came to see how my anger negatively impacted my friendships, created havoc at work, and put a strain on my marriage right from the beginning.

I entered into counseling to work through my "anger issues" and came to the conclusion that my behavior was a result of my environment and upbringing, and the solution was simply to manage my life better so that my fuse wouldn't run short. I *discovered my irritability triggers,* like too little sleep, being hungry, not getting through my to-do list, last minute change of plans, and did my best to *manage my lifestyle* in order to avoid an explosion.

But see, while I could "control" my time, I couldn't control others—especially when those "others" happened to be my children. Managing triggers simply wasn't enough when it came to avoiding my anger issues with my kids. And no matter how much I prayed and read my Bible, it seemed that my desire for the "gentle and quiet spirit" escaped my grasp. While I looked like the perfect Christian wife and momma on the outside, my heart was filled with disappointment and condemnation knowing how often I fell short behind closed doors.

By God's grace, my husband called me out on my ugly behavior at the same time the Lord was calling me to investigate the state of my heart.

That's when I ended up in counseling and poignantly discovered the essence of what was in my heart and giving way to what was coming out of my mouth (Matthew 12:33-35). My *heart was stored up with unforgiveness* toward my parents, bitterness over the dysfunction of my childhood, regret and shame over my rebellious years, fear of failure and a pursuit of perfection and people pleasing.

Yes, I was a mess and needed a spiritual heart transplant. By God's grace, that's exactly what He did. He healed my heart of every wound and made room for His love to fill every nook and cranny.

But was that enough to make my anger go away?

Yes. And no. The *change in my heart* led to a radical transformation in my behavior over the next few years. Enough of a change that my older girls noticed the difference and would comment, "Mom, why are you getting angry now? You don't do that any more!" But still, there was this part of me, on the inside, that wanted to rise up and spew ugly all too often and I've finally figured out why.

I was born this way. I was born angry!!

Not angry, as my mom thought. It's way more complicated than that. I believe God has wired me up like the poster child for the Choleric personality, which means I like to get things done, I see vision, I understand how to orchestrate situations to accomplish goals. Those are the lovely strengths of the Choleric.

It's the weaknesses, however, that seem to cause the problem, such as becoming easily angered, tending to use anger to manipulate, frustration when things don't move along fast enough, and preoccupation with achievement.

> *The way God made me is good—but if I'm not yielded to Him with my strengths and weaknesses, I'll make a mess of my life and my relationships.*

The fact is that I will always have a propensity toward anger, much like Paul's thorn in his side. But by God's grace, *anger doesn't have to control me.*

Through the power of the Holy Spirit at work in me, I can walk in step with the Spirit—sensitive to my triggers and surrendering to God my issues and frustrations—as I grow in trusting God with the things that seem to make me the most crazy.

This trusting God thing and looking at life from an eternal perspective really does help keep me calmer! And I know it can help you, too. I pray that if you're a born angry sister, you'll find hope in knowing that God made you for a good purpose, too. It's time to *embrace how you're made as you seek God* for any healing you need in your wounded heart and for the Holy Spirit to come alive within you, so that you may walk in His ways, especially as a mom whose kids may one day say, "Mom, you don't get angry like that any more!"

Response

1. What part of Elisa's story resonated with you?

2. How would you identify your "triggers?"

3. Take a moment and read Proverbs 4:23. Some people attempt to just protect their heart from "external" influences. But the Bible reminds us that we can never fully protect our heart "externally" because sin is something internal. We cannot overcome sin unless we uncover our hearts.

4. As Elisa mentioned, it was her husband that helped uncover unresolved hearts issues in her life. How can trusted and honest friends be a support to you in your journey to overcome sinful emotions?

Day 19

Don't Let Anger Destroy Your Family!
by Angela Richter at Together With Family

I had a couple of big milestones happen a few years ago. I turned 40 and celebrated my 20-year wedding anniversary.

> *If there is one thing looking back on my parenting and marriage that I regret the most, it has been my anger issues.*

Several years ago I was listening to a speaker talk about dealing with a difficult child and how he (the father) was angry all the time. He lost his temper easily, said hurtful words, and had become very controlling. He talked about the damage that had done to his family and as I walked out of the room, uncontrollable sobs took over my body. The Holy Spirit was convicting me and through this man's testimony I saw ME!

I came from a home of yellers, when I got married I couldn't believe how passive my husband was in this department. He was NOT a yeller but I was and I did it often. There was always guilt after a big blow out, but it didn't seem to make me not do it again.

It wasn't long after hearing the man's testimony that I heard a radio broadcast about a survey given to school children. They were asked if they could change one thing about their mom what would they change?

Guess what the majority said?

That she wouldn't yell so much. Ouch! Once again, God was convicting my spirit and I pulled over the car and repented.

But I still struggled!

A few years later my husband told me he was struggling in our marriage. Divorce has never been an option for us but I knew the anger issues had taken its toll, and I knew it had to change. Many times my anger was over what I thought were "big issues" but I will admit many times it was for very smallones. IwasmoredeterminedthanEVERtochangeit. IvowedafteraverypainfultalkthatI would never be the same.

The saddest thing to me was no one else ever saw my anger. They saw only the good parts. I started to realize everyone else thought so highly of me. They saw my love of the Lord Jesus, my church work, my commitment and an encouraging spirit, however my own family was living with an angry woman too much of the time.

So I began to change. I made a decision that day that I would do everything in my power to *not be angry anymore* and what wasn't in my power I would give to Jesus!

I am happy to say that I am not an angry woman anymore. There has been a huge transformation in my life, my marriage and in my home! My whole family has seen it and I have a *more peaceful and joyful spirit*. It is not always easy and it takes real work to overcome it but I am living proof it can be done!

Steps you can take if you have anger issues:

1. Prayer. God has to change your heart. Go to HIM daily over your anger issues. HE is the healer of your heart. It doesn't matter if you just repented yesterday, and you mess up again. Go to HIM anyway. He loves you so much and his GRACE never runs out!

2. Seek forgiveness from the ones you have hurt. I went to each child after begging my husband for forgiveness (which he graciously gave). I spoke to each of them about my anger issue and how I was going to change it. Children are so loving and so forgiving.

3. *Time out.* Don't hesitate to take a time out. I now will go in my room (I announce I'm taking a break) and lock the door. Take this time to pray, cry, and just take deep breaths. This is a *wonderful example to your children* (they see you are taking steps to control your struggles)

4. *Talk to someone.* See a counselor (there is no shame in that) or get an accountability partner. Find someone you can call when you think you might go over the line with your anger! Ask them to pray for you! Sometimes there is deep hurt from a painful past or *something else that causes anger.*

Remember the Bible said "Be angry and do not sin; do not let the sun go down on your anger." Ephesians 4:26: ESV I held on to this verse many times. If I use my tongue to say mean or hurtful things, that is indeed sinning!

Don't Let Anger Destroy Your Family!

Anger really can destroy the ones you love the most, but you can overcome it. It will take true commitment, prayer, and determination but you can do it. Your family is depending on it!

Response

1. In what ways is anger affecting your family?

2. Take a moment and read Matthew 5:21-26. What does Jesus associate anger with?

3. What does Jesus command when there is unresolved anger between people?

4. Based on this passage, how would summarize the danger of anger in relationships?

Day 20

Lessons from the Mustard Mess
(What To Do With Your Anger)
by Shannon McKee at In A Mirror Daily

The battle for my heart was finally calming as I kneeled over the soapy bucket. Steamy wisps came from the surface of the hot water as I surveyed the mess and began the job of mopping up the mustard that had splattered across the kitchen floor.

Yellow flecks had found their way onto the walls. And the woodwork. And the cabinets. The white cabinets. (Oh, yes, girls, bright yellow mustard does stain white woodwork...in case you're wondering.)

Humility was finally replacing rage as I scrubbed. And I wondered, was I really just wiping up the mustard or trying to erase my sin?

For I knew it now. There was no escaping the reality of it. I had done this thing. I had shattered the mustard bottle by throwing it to the ground in an angry outburst. It wasn't the kids and their bickering. Or our busy schedule. Or the reminder that I need to make another trip to the grocery store. Or the spazzy dog making noise in the background. Or even the fact that I was the only one who seemed to care about getting everything gathered up to go to the lake for the afternoon.

It might have looked like one of those things was to blame but it really wasn't. And I knew it.

It was me. I had done this thing. No one else.

What words had gone flying out of my mouth and into their tiny souls as I screamed at them and threw the mustard to the ground? What had I said when I slammed the kitchen door and stomped down the basement steps for extra emphasis? I couldn't remember now but I knew they hadn't been pretty. They certainly hadn't been the grace filled, life giving words of a woman controlled and empowered by the Spirit of God. Something else had replaced them. Something from the old ways. Something more like condemnation and selfishness and exasperation. *Something ugly.* And those words had spewed all over my kitchen too—probably making a bigger mess than the mustard stains.

Now the soapy water on the floor was mingling with fresh tears from these eyes and I finally stopped my scrubbing and just wept. In that moment, I gave up trying to scour away my own sin and let His blood cover over the mustard instead.

I shouldn't have been surprised when, right there in the mustard mess of my own doing, He joined me on the kitchen floor.

Isn't that the beauty of the Gospel? In that *moment of one of my grossest failures, God came in.* And instead of telling me to "keep calm and carry on," the God of the universe whispered, "keep humble and lean in." Because there wasn't anything calm about the mess I had just made. He wasn't going to dress it up. He also wasn't asking me to just suck it up and carry on like nothing had ever happened. No. He was just asking me to lean. To lean into the riches of His glorious grace. He was urging me to let the grace and favor that He had already purchased at the Cross pour over my weary head and wash through my home. It was the only thing that could truly clean up the mess I had made.

In the years that have followed my mustard moment, I've been learning:

It's less about how hard I try and more
about how hard I lean.

Maybe that sounds like a cop out. But I think it's one of the hardest things I've ever done. It's a tough concept in our 3 step, try harder culture. We American Christians don't know much about leaning. We live in the land of plenty where men are self made and books about being successful are in every home. What we know is trying harder.

Don't get me wrong, I'm not saying that all "trying" is bad. I'm not giving up on self control and discipline. Because I know I play a part in my growth and holiness. In that sense, I do "try." But, it's a responsive try.

I'm more convinced than ever that it's this leaning that is the answer. I need to *let the truth of the Gospel soak deep down* into every nook and cranny of my heart. I need the fruit of the Spirit to *manage my emotions*. I need God to help me turn from those idols that feed my anger in the first place. I also need Gospel induced grace and mercy to bring healing when I forget to lean...and fail instead.

So, I come to you humble. Not standing proud as one who has it all together with her supermom cape flying behind her as she tackles life undaunted. I come humble. As a mom who is convinced that leaning is the best posture.

And I have a few stubborn mustard flecks on cabinets to remind me of it.

Response

1. Have you ever had a mustard moment? How did you respond?

2. Take a moment and read John 15:4-5. What does it mean to "remain" or "abide" in Jesus?

3. What promise does Jesus offer in this passage?

Day 21
Before Mama Blows Her Stack
by Rachel Wojnarowski at RachelWojo.com

I honestly wish I could tell you I never get upset at my children. But I do.

He forgot his homework. Again.

She failed to mention the birthday party until the day of.

His clothes are all over the floor. For the tenth day in a row.

You see, being a parent is a 24/7 gig. Jesus said we would have trouble in this world, but man, no one told me it would come in the form of little self replicas who walk the earth, holding my heart.

Maybe *you're the mom who yells and gets it out of her system,* then feels horrible and must apologize.

Or perhaps you're more like me and the frustration eats away at your joy, occasionally permitting a slammed cabinet or irritated look.

No matter your expression or lack of in the anger department, we all know: If Mama ain't happy, ain't nobody happy.

> *For as she thinks in her heart, so is she.*
> *~Proverbs 23:7*

To *prevent those initial feelings of grumpiness*, I've asked the Lord to change my thought process. Before negative feelings have a chance to take hold, I'm tackling them in my mind first.

Allowing the upsetting issue to ruminate in my thought life only makes me more likely to act on those negative feelings. We can't always control how we feel about an issue, but we can control how we react to the issue. (Hmmm. Thinking I learned this from Lysa TerKeurst in a totally awesome book, *Unglued*. Highly recommend it.)

By this time, we've experienced some incredible advice on moving from grumpy to great here at The Better Mom! Today I wanted to explore how mama needs to think before she blows her stack.

When I analyzed what I thought about certain issues, then I discovered that by changing what I think before the issue occurs, I can more easily control my reaction to the negative issue.

For example, when I finish cleaning the kitchen, instead of thinking:

There—I'm finished with the kitchen. Hope no one comes in and messes it up.

I think:

It's ready to be used again!

Because we all know that it's going to be dirty again. Quite possibly within the next 2 minutes.

By placing a simple positive outlook on the completed task, we are changing the probability of our response to doing the same task again. While I haven't refined this process to perfection, when I stay in God's Word and think the right things, I've found I'm able to offer more positive reactions to negative situations.

Finally, brothers, whatever is true, whatever is honorable, whatever is just, whatever is pure, whatever is lovely, whatever is commendable, if there is any excellence, if there is anything worthy of praise, think about these things. Phil. 4:8

Response:

1. What stood out to you the most from today's chapter?

2. Take a moment and read 2 Timothy 1:7. Based on this verse, what does God's Spirit produce in us?

3. Sometimes fear and anger are the result of undisciplined thoughts or a mind that lacks self control. What are some practical ways we can "train" our thoughts?

4. Take a moment and read Philippians 4:8. How does this verse relate to controlling your thought life?

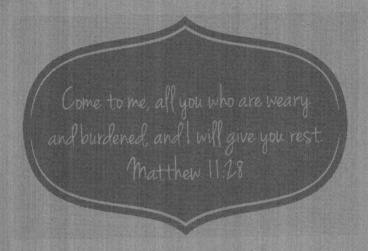

Come to me, all you who are weary
and burdened, and I will give you rest.
Matthew 11:28

Day 22
What Every Weary Mom Needs to Know
by Ruth Schwenk at TheBetterMom.com

The youngest of my four children is almost five years old, and I feel as if I am finally able to breathe (a little). However, I do remember those days of exhaustion—those sleepless nights which made it a struggle just to get through the day...especially when the days included battles with strongwilled children.

Like when I walked into the kitchen to find my oldest daughter carefully pouring a thin stream of lemonade. In an artful line. Around the ENTIRE. PERIMETER. of the kitchen FLOOR. Or when this same child would stand at the point where the hardwood floor and the carpet met, one foot in the kitchen and the other in the dining room (where food was forbidden), holding a glass of juice over the carpet, pushing herself (and me!) to the very edge of insanity.

Yes...moments such as these blurred into the next and into the next...and suddenly days and weeks had passed in a hazy fog. Needless to say, I was definitely a physically weary mom. Adding to the fatigue was the *emotionally taxing devastation of pregnancies followed by miscarriages...five times!*

So let me be the first to admit that total and complete exhaustion—both of the physical and emotional variety—makes me grumpy, makes me act out, and makes me withdraw. How about you? Here are a few bits of wisdom...things I wish someone would have shared with me during those demanding days...

Things Every Weary Mom Needs to Know

1. Steal moments with God. I say steal, because we all know that with small children running around, you will literally have to snatch moments when you can get them! Keep your Bible on the kitchen counter to read a passage as you prepare dinner; get up before your children to pray; read scripture out loud to your kids at meal time; post scripture on the bathroom mirror or on the laundry room wall. Whenever possible, *get into the Bible and talk to God.*

2. Lean into the work. Mothering is hard work. Period. Why do we fight that? Instead, we must lean into the labor, understanding that shaping hearts demands diligence and persistence, care and attention. There is nothing easy about it. Welcome the calling, expect it to be challenging and enjoy the journey.

3. Find an encouraging friend. Share this time in community with another mom or two who can lend support and cheer, and even inspiration and example. It will double your joy and divide your pain.

4. Embrace the motherhood mission. In her book aptly titled *The Mission of Motherhood*, Sally Clarkson says, "Saying yes to the mission of motherhood has certainly not meant giving up my ministry. To a great extent, it is my ministry!" When we see our very own children in our very own homes as our very own special ministry from God, amazing growth takes place...in our children and in us.

Friends, *God picked you to shepherd your precious children,* and that gives you great responsibility and deep purpose. My prayer is that—on those especially draining days—these few suggestions might help you be a little less grumpy, a little less apt to act out, a little less prone to withdraw. I created this printable below as a reminder for you (and me)!

Hang in there, Mama. You can do this!

1. In what ways are you physically taxed as a mother?

2. Take a moment and read 2 Timothy 2:1-7. What three types of people does the Apostle Paul use in this passage?

3. Each of these serves as examples of how we are to persevere in the work God has set before you. Describe how parenting is like the three people mentioned in the passage above:

Don't copy the behavior and customs of this world, but **let God** transform you into a

∽ new person ∾

by changing the way you think. Then you will learn to **know God's will** for you, which is **good** and **pleasing** and **perfect**.

Galatians 6:4-5 NLT

Day 23

I Don't Want to be an Angry Mom, So I Threw Away My Coffee Pot

by Jamerrill Stewart at Holy Spirit-Led Homeschooling

It was an extreme measure. I stood there looking at my white plastic framed appliance in the large black hefty bag.

I had thrown away my coffee pot.

In life we will face moments in which we have to draw a line in the sand and say no more. That was my coffee pot in the trash morning. I was done.

The morning had started out with noble intentions. It was Sunday and my family and I were in the normal fast paced mode of getting everyone ready. There are eight of us so the getting ready part is greatly multiplied. This particular morning I had poured myself my normal large cup of lovely coffee. And I always made my coffee like a dessert—no messing around here. In goes lots of sugar, flavored coffee creamer, topped with ready-whip out of the can and sprinkled with cinnamon.

Mmmmm, I can smell it now.

This particular Sunday morning as we rushed through our

morning I could feel the pressure mounting. As life flew at me I kept swigging my coffee.

Got one kid dressed. Gulp.

Directed other children to the table for cereal. Chug down more coffee.

Oh, wait it's 9 a.m., we need to leave by 9:30 and I'm not dressed yet. Sad, I can see the bottom of my cup.

I finished that cup so I went for a 2nd, because coffee makes me happy. By the time the 2nd cup was done we were nearly out the door. However, I didn't stop to eat. I hadn't had any water to drink. I knew that my mind, body, and soul function much better when I actually take care of myself, but I had gotten lazy again.

I knew I had gotten back into a *nasty habit of yelling* or at least raising my voice too much. When I feel overwhelmed I get moody and snappy which inevitability ends in me yelling like a nut.

Nearing our departure five of our six sweet children were in the living room getting on jackets and shoes. Now, I don't even remember the full dynamics of the situation, just that I was a mom with only caffeine in my veins and my children were being kids with only childhood in their veins.

I snapped.

A big, ugly, yelling, screaming, pressured mom snap. I yelled, best I can say, like a nut.

And they cried. Even my 12 year old cried.

Then I cried.

And I knew at that moment that I had to do something drastic because I obviously couldn't handle the amount of caffeine in my system.

On the way to church as I talked out the situation with my husband I reflected on how anytime I've really had a yelling outburst during my motherhood years it is usually directly related to me drinking too much coffee. I prayed about it in church and felt the Lord tell me to throw my coffee pot away. As soon as we got home I couldn't get the thing in the trash quick enough.

I went for several months without any caffeine and worked on making sure I ate well and drank plenty of water in the mornings. I also cut all sugars and refined carbohydrates from my diet.

Now, almost a year later, I enjoy a cup of coffee during my time with the Lord in the morning and I feel peace about drinking it with the additional diet and lifestyle changes that are in place. I had to *surrender that area of my life to the Lord* and follow Him in the adjustments that I desperately needed.

You may not have a problem with coffee. You may have another area that you need more discipline and control in. Just as I had to completely rid my body and home from coffee for a season you may have to purge some junk and hand certain areas to the Lord as you gain *victory in your life and mothering.*

Response

1. In what ways do you think a food or beverage can become a vice?

2. Take a moment and read Psalm 94:19. What does the psalmist say comforts or consoles him?

3. How do you know if you are depending on something other than God to provide your joy or strength?

4. While giving up coffee may be a personal decision, are there areas that you sense God leading you to give up to draw closer to Him?

Day 24

He Restores My Soul

by Jennifer Ebenhack at JeniferEbenhack.com

Jesus, I can't keep living like this. I'm being eaten alive.

I hate everyone. I'm exhausted. I'm desperate!

I'm afraid I'll do something horrible. God...you have to help me!

Tears poured down my face as I sat on my bed that fourth summer in Haiti. Without much hope, I opened the One Year Bible in my lap. I only had a few minutes before one or all five kids would find me. I looked through the blur at the words on the page.

Psalm 23

Sigh. I was hoping for some life changing verses I'd never noticed before. Oh well.

The Lord is my shepherd; I shall not want.

Well, I DO want. I'm not doing too well here.

He makes me to lie down in green pastures; He leads me beside the still waters.

Lie down? That sounds heavenly. In green pastures by still waters? Oh God, if only I could go there!

He restores my soul.

Pause. Reread.

He restores my soul.

I felt like I'd walked through the Sahara and was now invited into sparkling turquoise waters. Are you serious God? You can do that? Don't tease me!

One more time: *He restores my soul.*

The truth shook me to the core...my husband, friends, and family were powerless to perform the duties of my Savior—my Shepherd. I had placed impossible burdens on everyone around me. No wonder they'd failed to deliver.

Okay, Jesus. *Be my Shepherd.* Please, PLEASE restore my soul. Help me! I am such a mess!

As I prayed, I shifted my expectations off of the people around me, off of my demand for different circumstances, onto the shoulders of my Shepherd. I wept as I repented of my self-centeredness. I'd tried for months to prove to others the depths of my despair, but now I was released from that burden.

I was still on my bed, in a sweltering, cluttered room. *Nothing had changed, but everything had changed.* Spiritually I'd been plunged into those still, sparkling waters of restoration.

Half a moment later, there was a knock at the door. Someone needed me for something urgent, as always.

I wiped my wet cheeks, laid the Bible down, and walked toward the door. I knew this day would be full of tests and challenges. I knew my habits of resentment wouldn't die easily.

But I'd been reminded that God was real. His love was real, His Word was powerful and true, and *He was able to restore.*

He'd heard my cries.

Where are you today, friend? Are you looking to coffee, a shopping trip, more sensitivity from your husband, or an offer of help from your mom to restore you? As you battle irritation, crabbiness, or complete hopelessness today, turn to the tender Shepherd of your soul for restoration. Cry out to the One who leads the parched to still water!

Response

1. Take a moment and read John 4:1-15. What does Jesus promise the women at the well?

2. What does Jesus mean by "living water?"

3. Are there "wells" in your life that you keep drawing from that will never satisfy like the source of Living Water?

Make a careful exploration of who you are and the work you have been given, and then sink yourself into that.

~ Don't be impressed with yourself ~

Don't compare yourself with others. Each of you must take responsibility for doing the creative best you can with your own life.

Galatians 6:4-5 NLT

Don't copy the behavior and customs of this world, but **let God** transform you into a

~ new person ~

by changing the way you think. Then you will learn to **know God's will** for you, which is **good** and **pleasing** and **perfect**.

Galatians 6:4-5 NLT

Father, I confess that I have copied the behavior and customs of the world - specifically the custom of comparing myself to others. Forgive me!

Please, transform me into a new person by changing the way I think! I trust that you will teach me so that I can learn to know your will - your good and pleasing and perfect will.

Help me to carefully explore who I am and all the work You have given to me. Then, help me to sink myself into that work!

Forgive me for in any way being overly impressed with myself, and forgive me for comparing myself with others.

All of this comparing has prevented me from taking responsibility for doing the creative best I can with the life YOU have given me.

I love you, Jesus.

Amen!

Day 25

Six Strategies to Stop the Crabby Custom of Comparing

by Rhonda Owens

I am not supposed to compare myself to others...but I do it anyway.

It happens like a sneak attack on my less mentally tough turf—those areas in which I feel least confident.

For example, sometimes I feel that my life lacks purpose.

Therefore, when I begin the comparing game it is suddenly as if I am surrounded by wildly successful moms who not only have intensely influential careers out of which they impact the world, but also they have sixteen happy children all doing pinterest-worthy activities, doting husbands who love every single meal they prepare, clean and organized homes that run flawlessly, plans to adopt a couple more kids from an impoverished land, and objectives to build a hospital in the remote jungles of nowhere.

I'm exaggerating, but you get the idea: in short, it appears as if everyone else is living the (perfectly purposeful) dream...and I am not.

That's when I get crabby.

Instead of embracing the gifts God has given me, instead of

turning my attention to the plans He does have for me, instead of praying for wisdom and direction and peace...

I pout.

Can anyone relate?

Comparing makes us liars. We rarely compare apples to apples. Tricia Goyer, in her new book entitled *Balanced: Finding Center as a Work-at-Home-Mom*, says, "Too often we compare our weaknesses with other people's strengths only to find ourselves coming up short." We compare our worst to someone else's best which sets us up to sound like failures. Essentially, we begin lying to ourselves.

Comparing makes us selfish. We cop a "woe is me" attitude which is self focused and unbecoming. God commands us to love Him and to love others—both which become difficult when throwing a personal pity party.

Comparing makes us ungrateful. Like small children, we obsess over what someone else has and how it compares to what we don't have all the while forgetting to express gratitude for what we do have.

Lying, selfish, ungrateful people are CRABBY! We need to stop comparing.

Here are a few strategies to stop the crabby custom of comparing:

1. ***Renew your mind.*** Tempted to compare? Train your mind to confess it (I'm sorry for comparing her gifts with mine, God) and to credit Him for all He HAS given you (Thank you, God, for _____).

   We should not copy the behavior and customs of this world, but instead we should let God transform us into new people by changing the way we think. Then will we learn what God's will is for us (Romans 12:2 NLT).

   Note: this whole process happens in our minds!

2. Construct a question. If there is something you admire in another person, deflect the compulsion to compare by asking a question that sparks discussion: Could you tell me about your discipline strategy? What is your method for planning meals?

3. Listen for lessons. Observe the way another mom is doing something—disciplining a child, ordering her home, caring for her parents—and learn! God may have something to teach you through her example.

4. Implement HIS plan. Tricia Goyer says, "What truly matters is simply lifting our faces to heaven and asking, 'Lord, what do you think?'"

So. True.

We need to practice tuning out every voice but His.

5. Be YOUR best. Carefully explore the work you have been given, and sink yourselves into it. Instead of comparing yourself to others, take responsibility for doing the creative best you can with your own life (Galatians 6:4-5 MSG).

6. Pray the Word. Find a printable file in the printables section at the end of the book to help you with this step!

Girlfriends, comparing ourselves to one another is conventional in our culture, but with concerted effort we can curb this crabby custom!

Response

1. In what ways do I compare myself with others?

2. What does Philippians 4:4 say we are to do? How does rejoicing guard our hearts from comparison?

3. Take a moment and read Philippians 4:11-13. How is contentment a cure for being crabby?

4. What can you do practically to avoid the pitfall of comparing?

Day 26
Surrender
by Christy at One Fun Mom

Once upon a time I had a vision of motherhood.

It involved hilltops and harmony, sort of like *The Sound of Music*.

There was daily structure and soft sacrifices, like Caroline daily performed in the *Little House* books.

And for some reason, I envisioned lying on green grass, making cloud shapes with my little ones.

My ideals of motherhood did NOT involve grouchiness. Caroline Ingalls was never grouchy, Julie Andrews was never grouchy, and I certainly would not be grouchy either!

When I envisioned myself as a mother, I never envisioned God as part of my plan. I didn't need God in my plan. I was already put together!

Except I'm not.

I am grouchy. More often than I want to be.

And all too often I decide I'm going to fix my grouchiness. I'm going to pull myself together. I'm going to give it one more try.

Except I can't.

Motherhood has a way of bringing us to the feet of Jesus like nothing else.

*Motherhood brings us to the end of ourselves
and pushes us one...tiny...bit...further.*

If we don't learn to surrender to Jesus, if we don't learn to stop trying and start resting, this motherhood business will chew us up and spit us out.

We need to bring God back into our mothering. He needs to come before our homemaking binders and DIY improvement projects and fancy schedules. These things will not help us with our failings. We cannot do it on our own.

These words are on my heart like no other. I have lived in the valley of trying. I have prayed and sought God on the surface, but deep down relied on myself. I know the futility of our attempts at control first hand.

To begin to release our anger and grouchiness, we must release ourselves to God.

Surrender.

And the most beautiful thing is,that's all God asks of us.
He is waiting.

*Behold, I stand at the door and knock. If anyone hears
My voice and opens the door, I will come in to him
and dine with him, and he with Me.
~Revelation 3:20*

Response

1. How would you describe surrender?

2. Take a moment and read 2 Corinthians 5:14-15. In your own words, summarize these two verses.

3. When we choose not to surrender, we are really fighting God for control. We desire to be in charge of the present and the future. How has the lack of surrender caused you unhealthy emotions?

4. In what areas do you need to hand over control to God?

Be joyful in hope, patient in affliction,
faithful in prayer.
Romans 12:12

Resources

From all of us at The Better Mom, thank you for joining us on this journey! Again, we pray that this is a resource that is helpful for you in your walk with Christ. If you are interested in further study, we invite you to subscribe to *The Better Mom* online community at *thebettermom.com* and receive free downloadable gifts plus a list of our most popular resources to further support your *Grouchy to Great* journey.

The Contributors

Angela Richter

Angela is a wife and work at home homeschooling mom to three children. She is a speaker and a blogger who has a real heart for encouraging moms in homeschooling, parenting, and connecting with their children. You can find Angela at Together with Family (*www.togetherwithfamily.com*).

Brooke McGlothlin

Brooke is a mom of two young boys who leave her desperate for grace, knowing that if God doesn't show up...nothing happens. She's the co-author of *Hope for the Weary Mom: Where God Meets You in Your Mess*, and her newest book, *Praying for Boys: Asking God for the Things They Need Most*, from Bethany House Publishers. She helps moms find delight in the chaos of raising boys as co-founder of the M.O.B. Society (*www.themobsociety.com*).

Christin Slade

Christin is wife of 13+ years to her high school sweetheart and mother to seven children. She sees beauty in the simple things and appreciates a good cup of coffee. She is learning to live everyday with joy, find gratitude in the mundane, and speak words of grace. You can find Christin writing through her days on Joyful Mothering, encouraging writing moms and hanging out on Google+.

Carlie Kercheval

Carlie Kercheval is a happily married stay-at-home homeschooling mom. She and her college sweetheart have been blessed with 3 precious children to raise while traveling the world as a military family. Carlie is the founder of Today's Frugal Mom (*todaysfrugalmom. com*), So You Call Yourself a Homeschooler? and Managing Your Blessings. She is also the co-author of the Learning to Speak Life (*www.learningtospeaklife.com*) family Bible studies and co-host of the Learning to Speak Life Radio Show. When she is not busy enjoying her family and the great outdoors, you can typically find her cozied up somewhere under a blanket with a good book. You can connect with her on Facebook, Pinterest, and Twitter.

Christy Halsell

Christy is the mother of four boys and one girl. She has been known to homeschool, change diapers and potty train simultaneously. She's been married for 11 years to Charlie, a surfer and entrepreneur and lives on the Central Coast of California. Christy's passion is to embrace motherhood as the calling God gave her. In the midst of the hard work mothering requires, she strives for new ways to have a fun outlook on being a mother. She shares her ideas and encouragement at One Fun Mom (*www.onefunmom.com*).

Denise

Denise is an author, columnist, wife and home educating mom of three boys. Together with her family she resides in the beautiful Pacific Northwest, where her desire is to live a simple life that honors God and family. You can find her blogging at Little House on the Valley (*littlehouseonthevalley.com*) where she loves to inspire women to flourish within their hearts and homes.

Daniele Evans

Daniele of Domestic Serenity (*www.domesticserenity.org*) is a homeschooling Mama of five kiddos and a voracious reader of books. Passionate about her faith, home and family, she blogs about the intentional lifestyle and writes for other online and print publications. Daniele thinks life is made more enjoyable with a cup of herbal tea in hand!

Elisa Pulliam

Elisa Pulliam is passionate about women experiencing a life transformed by God for the sake of impacting the next generation—a mission fueled by God's redeeming work in her life and twenty plus years in youth and women's ministry. She's the author of *Meet the New You: A 21 Day Plan for Embracing Fresh Attitudes and Focused Habits for Real Life Change*, which is a book designed to help women embrace a fresh encounter with God, and *Impact Together: Biblical Mentoring Simplified*. She is also founder of *moretobe.com* and tremendously enjoys working as a life coach and coach trainer. She considers her greatest roles as wife to Stephen and mom to four amazing children. Connect with Elisa at *elisapulliam.com*.

Jennifer Ebenhack

Jennifer is the author of *Take Courage: Choosing Faith on My Journey of Fear*, and blogs at *jenniferebenhack.com*. She and her husband Jarod served as missionaries in the country of Haiti, where they became parents to all five of their children, three of whom are adopted. Those eventful years produced a gift of brokenness in Jennifer through which she has discovered the depths of God's healing grace.

In between loads of laundry, homeschooling, and enjoying the South Florida shoreline she is writing a memoir of their nine year adoption process and eight years in Haiti.

Jennifer Smith

Jennifer married her best friend Aaron in January of 2007. They jumped straight into missions living in three different states and three different countries during their first two years of marriage. Her passion for missions, writing, and marriage led her to create Unveiled Wife (*www.unveiledwife.com*), where she blogs about being a wife with every intention to inspire other wives to develop God-centered marriages. Her and her husband are expecting their first child later this year. You can find Jennifer on Twitter and join the Unveiled Wife Community on Facebook (*bit.ly/2g7sPHu*).

Jessica Smartt

Jessica Smartt used to be a librarian and an English teacher, but now she works much harder just being a mom. You can find her blogging at "Smartter" Each Day (*www.smarttereachday.com*) where she pokes fun at the everyday challenges of motherhood, shares all her delicious allergy-free recipes, and rejoices that God loves her no matter what phobia she's recently developed. She is blessed to the moon and back with two energetic little boys and a husband who actually never worries.

Jamerrill Stewart

Jamerrill Stewart has been married to her best friend Travis for 15 years. They make their home in the gorgeous Shenandoah Valley where they are raising 6 beautiful babies (baby, 2, 4, 7, 10, 13) for Jesus. Jamerrill has a passion to help families afford the homeschool life; she does so each day by providing homeschool freebies, deals, and encouragement at Free Homeschool Deals (*www. freehomeschooldeals.com*). She is also the creator of Holy Spirit-led Homeschooling (*www.holyspiritledhomeschooling.net*) where families encourage one another to live the life of faith.

Kate Battistelli

Kate is blessed to be married to Mike, her best friend! She's mom to recording artist Francesca Battistelli and adores being Mimi to Franny's two children, 3 year old Eli and 1 year old Audrey Jane. Kate's a Jersey girl currently living in Atlanta and passionate about two things: Encouraging women to believe there is a Big God-sized plan for your family and sharing recipes and techniques helping you cook healthy, delicious meals for your family using whole foods and organic ingredients. She's the author of *Growing Great Kids: Partner with God to Cultivate His Purpose in Your Child's Life*, published by Charisma House and she blogs about food and faith at *KateBattistelli.com*. Follow her on Twitter, Instagram and Facebook.

Kara Chupp

Kara is 17 years married to her husband Jason, one of the funniest and most generous people she knows. They have five kiddos, four here and one in heaven. They also have a muppet-like-mess of a dog, non-breeding Madagascar Hissers (who have had over 100 babies), guinea pigs, and a whole bunch of stick bugs. Kara writes mostly about family, adoption, grief, education, traditions, literature, organization, Heaven—and most importantly—her love for God. You can find her at *KaraChupp.com*.

Lisa Jacobson

Lisa is the happily-ever-after wife of Matt Jacobson, literary agent and author, and together they enjoy raising and home educating their 8 children. She's also rather fond of dark chocolate, French press coffee, and deep friendships (though not necessarily in that order). She encourages women to embrace the rich life of loving relationships and the high calling of being a wife and mother. You can find her sharing her passion for husband, home, and family over at Club31Women (club31women.com) and on Facebook

Take a look at her new book: *100 Ways to Love Your Husband* (*amzn.to/2gJeUZt*).

Natalie Falls

Natalie Is a wife to her best friend and mother to her three children. God changed Natalie's perspective on life when her son, Elias, was born with Down syndrome. She is passionate about writing, photography, and giving hope to others. You can find inspiration as Natalie blogs about her journey of motherhood and life at *nataliefalls.com*. Follow her on Instagram, Facebook, and Twitter.

Rhonda Owens

Gifted with one beautiful daughter for her tenth wedding anniversary and another for her twentieth, high school English teacher turned freelance writer/homeschooling mom Rhonda Owens is thrilled to be back in the "writing saddle" again. Previously, her work appeared in such publications as CCM Magazine, Christian Retailing, Inspirational Giftware, Memory Makers Magazine, and Boundless. org among others. Passionate about the Word, Rhonda loves nothing more than to study scripture, talk about it, write about it, apply it, live it and teach it...all preferably accompanied by deep community and good chocolate.

Ruth Schwenk

Ruth Schwenk is the founder of The Better Mom (*thebettermom. com*), and along with her husband, the creator of For the Family. She is a pastor's wife, mom of four energetic kids, a lover of coffee, and dreamer of big dreams. She loves leading, speaking, and blogging. Ruth is the co-author of *Hoodwinked: Ten Myths Moms Believe and Why We All Need to Knock It Off* (*amzn.to/1SHhT3m*)and *Pressing Pause: 100 Quiet Moments for Moms to Meet With Jesus* (*amzn.to/1Pxcyvg*). A graduate of The Moody Bible Institute, Ruth and her husband have been in fulltime church ministry for over fifteen years.

Ruth Simons

Ruth is the author of Gracelaced (*www.gracelaced.com*)where she writes about finding grace in the everyday life. Her days are filled with 6 energetic boys, whom she homeschools parttime through the Classical school her husband heads and co-founded. She has recently transitioned out of her 10 year role as a Pastor's wife through which she has consistently learned this marvelous truth that keeps her going each and every day: The Lord is not through with us yet.

Ruth Soukup

Ruth Soukup is a writer, photographer, DIY-er, food-lover, proud wife and mama, and a child of God, saved by grace. Her passion is her family and creating a home filled with joy and purpose. Her blog Living Well Spending Less (*www.livingwellspendingless.com*) follows her adventure of finding the Good Life on a budget, a journey that began after her spending became so out-of-control that her marriage was on the brink of collapse. Eventually she has discovered that not only does she enjoy saving money, but that a life well lived is not about what we have, but who we are. She lives in SW Florida with her husband and two daughters.

Rachel Wojnarowski

Rachel Wojnarowski is a wife, mom to 7, blogger, writer and speaker. She and her husband, Matt, enjoy caring for their busy family, whose ages span 2 years to 22 years and includes a special needs daughter. In her "free time" she crochets, knits, and sews handmade clothing. Ok, not really. She enjoys running and she's a tech geek at heart. Rachel teaches social media and blogging classes in her local community and also speaks at Christian women conferences. Wife, mom, reader, writer, speaker and dreamer, you can find Rachel at *RachelWojo.com*.

Shannon McKee

Shannon is a self-proclaimed putterer. She likes to dabble in this, that, and the other thing. Sometimes that creates a lot of inner turmoil and lost productivity. But, it gives her a lot to write about at her blog In a Mirror Dimly. She feels blessed to be able to write from home, directing some online publicity for a local firm in Northeast Ohio. Some things that move her: loving her Pastor-husband and their two kiddos, supporting the public school her kids attend, sharing hospitality and creating refuge, living missional, and teaching women to study the Bible. That, AND devouring dark chocolate almonds from Trader Joe's.

Tricia Goyer

Tricia Goyer is a busy mom of ten, grandmother of two, and wife to John. Somewhere around the hustle and bustle of family life, she manages to find the time to write fictional tales delighting and entertaining readers and non-fiction titles offering encouragement and hope. A bestselling author, Tricia has published fifty books to date and has written more than 500 articles. She is a two time Carol Award winner, as well as a Christy and ECPA Award Nominee. To connect with Tricia go to *TriciaGoyer.com* or *Facebook.com/AuthorTriciaGoyer*.

Tune in to *The Better Mom* podcast with Ruth Schwenk and friends. as we **gather** together, **grow** as women and in turn **give** the best of who we are to our families.

The Better Mom: Growing in Grace between Perfection and the Mess releases April 2018! In The Better Mom, popular blogger, pastor's wife and mother of four, Ruth Schwenk, reminds us that Jesus calls us to live not a weary life, but a worthy life. As a mom we don't have to settle for either being apathetic or struggling to be perfect. Both visions of motherhood go too far. Ruth offers a better option. She says, "It's okay to come as we are, but what we're called to do and be is far too important to stay there! The way to becoming a better mom starts not with what we are doing, but with who God is inviting us to become." Available everywhere books are sold.

Made in the USA
Middletown, DE
02 May 2018